# living well, dying well
## A Study of Euthanasia and End-of-Life Issues

FAITH
ALIVE®
Christian Resources

Grand Rapids, Michigan

Faith Alive wishes to thank the following sources for making this study possible:

- The Committee for Contact with the Government (Canada), which originally prepared this report to respond to government initiatives related to euthanasia.

- The authors of this report, Louisa Bruinsma, Reinder Klein, Rudy Ouwehand, and Jack Westerhof, who submitted this report, originally titled *The Report of the Committee for Contact with the Government (Canada) Regarding Responsibility and Community at the End of Life*, to Synod 2000 of the Christian Reformed Church in North America.

- Louis M. Tamminga, who adapted this report for church education, group, and individual study.

Unless otherwise noted, the Scripture quotations in this publication are taken from the HOLY BIBLE, NEW INTERNATIONAL VERSION, © 1973, 1978, 1984, International Bible Society. Used by permission of Zondervan Bible Publishers.

Faith Alive Christian Resources published by CRC Publications.
*Living Well, Dying Well: A Study of Euthanasia and End-of-Life Issues,* © 2001, CRC Publications, 2850 Kalamazoo Ave. SE, Grand Rapids, MI 49560. All rights reserved. Printed in the United States of America on recycled paper. ♻

We welcome your comments. Call us at 1-800-333-8300 or e-mail us at editors@faithaliveresources.org.

**Library of Congress Cataloging-in-Publication Data**
Living well, dying well: a study of euthanasia and end-of-life issues.
    p. cm.
    "The contents of this booklet faithfully represent what the Christian Reformed Synod of 2000 wanted to contribute to the discussion surrounding end-of-life issues"—Preface.
    Includes bibliographical references.
    ISBN 1-56212-798-5
    1. Euthanasia—Religious aspects—Christianity. 2. Euthanasia—Moral and ethical aspects—Christianity. 3. Medical ethics—Religious aspects—Christianity. I. Christian Reformed Church.
R726.L56   2001
241'.697—dc21

                           2001033500

10 9 8 7 6 5 4 3 2 1

# contents

# preface

None of us can avoid dealing with the subject matter of this booklet. It addresses death and dying and end-of-life issues. We need each other in living. We also need each other in the process of dying.

In this booklet the church wants to talk with believers about these issues, because it's not only very important how we live but also how we die.

The contents of this booklet faithfully represent what the Christian Reformed Synod of 2000 wanted to contribute to the discussion surrounding end-of-life issues and the church's ministry to those who are dying, their loved ones, and those who provide them with care. The report is reproduced here in a slightly modified format. In order to facilitate personal and group study we have divided it into eight sections, adding some discussion helps, questions, and explanatory notes to help you in your study and discussion. You can find the actual report in the *Christian Reformed Church in North America Agenda for Synod 2000*, pages 425-448. Synod's response to the report, including some minor revisions (which have been incorporated here), is in the *Christian Reformed Church in North America Acts of Synod 2000*, pages 685-686, 706-709, and 724.

May your thoughtful reflections on these materials enrich your life and help you in preparing for your life's end with grace. May this report equip and motivate you to minister to those who are approaching the last chapter of life. And may it help you to witness to the light of God's Word and will within our society.

—Louis M. Tamminga

# introduction

## How Synods Offer Pastoral Advice

In the Christian Reformed Church, synods are yearly, week-long meetings of church representatives from across the continent who set policy and make decisions for the denomination. These meetings focus on decision making. Most of the items on the synodical agenda originate with the regional groups of churches called classes. So a classis is one of forty-seven regions in the United States and Canada. Whenever classes deal with issues they cannot resolve, or with issues that concern the denomination as a whole, they will have them placed on the agenda of the annual synod. Synod is composed of delegates from the classes—each classis sends four delegates.

Sometimes synod deals with pastoral matters of real importance to the churches. To communicate its pastoral advice effectively, synod sometimes asks CRC Publications, its publishing arm, to print such material in a booklet for easy study access. This booklet is one outcome of this process. In providing this advice, synod wishes not only to reach members of the Christian Reformed Church in North America but also to engage others within and beyond the community of faith as well. So whether you are a member of the CRC or of another church, or are a health care provider, government legislator, or an individual who is just plain interested in this issue, we pray that you will receive help and direction from your study of this report.

## The Origins of This Report

The origin of this pastoral advice offered by Synod 2000 had some unusual elements. Synod 1993 considered a brief report submitted by the Council of Christian Reformed Churches in Canada, an umbrella organization for its Canadian classes. The Council's Committee for Contact with the Government had for some years been involved in end-of-life issues as these surfaced in the public arena of Canadian life. The Canadian Parliament had considered the possibility of legalizing euthanasia ("mercy-killing") and assisted suicide. The Canadian government

7

held public hearings across the land and invited Canadians to express their views by submitting briefs and position papers. The Committee for Contact with the Government used the opportunity to submit a paper, copies of which were sent to all Christian Reformed congregations in Canada.

Subsequently Classis Chatham asked Synod 1997 to appoint a study committee to "determine an appropriate denominational position with respect to the practice of euthanasia." One of the grounds that classis added to its proposal was that a carefully considered position would guide the churches in their witness in society. In its request, Classis Chatham referred specifically to the testimony of the Committee for Contact with the Government to the Canadian government, entitled "Medical Decisions and Public Policy Pertaining to the End-of-Life."

Synod 1997 did not appoint a study committee. Instead, it asked the Committee for Contact with the Government to broaden its study to include exegetical material and practical implications of biblical principles for persons making decisions about death and dying. Synod asked that copies be sent to the churches in Canada and the United States for evaluation and discussion.

The Committee for Contact with the Government submitted its finished product to Synod 2000. The report not only reflected on the public side of end-of-life issues (such as legislation governing medical practices) but also on how churches can best minister to people struggling with terminal illness and people facing imminent death.

The report is biblical in its approach and sensitive to the needs of suffering and dying persons and to the needs of people ministering to them. Consider, for example, these paragraphs from the report:

> At the very outset we as a committee affirm our commitment to the life God has granted us. We know that sorrow or pain, indignity or frustration may make that life a heavy burden for some. Yet we believe that suicide and mercy killing are not appropriate responses to the anguish and despair that life sometimes brings. And so the challenge before the committee was to develop and propose responses—both personal and communal—that *are* appropriate when Christians are confronted with end-of-life questions and situations. This report attempts to

help Christians make biblically informed decisions pertaining to the end of life, play an active and positive role . . . in the ongoing public discussions on the subject, and ensure that our church will become an effective and compassionate community of care for persons in the dying stage of life.

This report is essentially about life. Our desire as a committee, arising out of a biblically and confessionally based respect for the gift of life, is to help Christians face the challenges that accompany the approaching end of life, though we could not specifically address every aspect of the many and complicated issues surrounding the process of dying and of medical treatment in the final stages of life.

*—Acts of Synod 2000, p. 425*

## How to Use This Booklet

We have split the Committee's report into manageable sections and in the margin added some tips, questions, and discussion starters. We hope you will find these useful in guiding your study. If you are reading this on your own, take some time to reflect on them. If you are using this report in a group study, you might want to use one or two sections for each of your sessions. Don't be afraid to skip those you find less relevant to your situation. Your group does not need to discuss or answer every question; instead, choose the questions that are of real interest to your participants. And don't forget to spend some time in prayer, asking God to grant you wisdom, obedience, and love as you tackle these issues and intercede diligently for those who so intensely need life's Author and Sustainer as they face the end of their own lives or of those they love.

# recent cases involving end-of-life decisions

*The committee presented the following actual end-of-life–related cases. These cases demonstrate how important end-of-life issues have become both in the experience of individuals and in public administration.*

## Two Opposite Responses

*Oregon, 1997*

In April 1997 two Oregon patients legally took their own lives with the aid of medical doctors. These were the first physician-assisted suicides in the United States after the Oregon state legislature enacted a law permitting doctors to prescribe lethal drugs for the purpose of ending a person's life. It is a law that, in effect, condones assisted suicide.

*Michigan*

No other state has followed Oregon's example, not even Michigan, where pathologist Dr. Jack Kevorkian has, by his own admission, assisted in over 130 similar deaths. As a matter of fact, Michigan simply had no legislation on the matter until recently, although a 1994 Michigan State Supreme Court ruling held that common law prohibited the practice. That ruling was later upheld by a federal court, a fact that makes it even more remarkable that until the spring of 1999 no jury would convict Dr. Kevorkian. He was convicted of murder in the spring of 1999. In September 1998 a new law (SB200) intended to "amend the Michigan penal code to prohibit and provide penalties for assisting in a suicide or attempted suicide," took effect. The bill was introduced and sponsored by state Senator William Van Regenmorter, a member of the Christian Reformed Church.

The role played by ordinary citizens in Oregon and Michigan is instructive. In both states the issue was considered so fraught with complex moral and ethical dimensions that

The referendums held in Oregon and Michigan had opposite outcomes. Oregon allowed assisted suicide while Michigan forbade it. What could explain the difference?

Should we make a distinction between personal and public morals? How would you respond to someone who argues that your objection to assisted suicide stems from your own personal moral convictions and that therefore you should not impose those convictions on your fellow citizens?

Are there circumstances in which you believe euthanasia might be justified? Explain.

elected officials chose to leave the matter up to the people. Both state legislatures chose to settle the question of physician-assisted suicide by referendum. The results were strikingly different. In Oregon the people voted to support the end-of-life referendum, Measure 51, by a 60 percent to 40 percent vote (Nov. 1997). Oregon thus became the first jurisdiction in the United States to permit doctors to actively and intentionally help dying persons end their own lives. The people of Michigan, however, defeated Proposition B—a proposal that would have made physician-assisted suicide legal in their state—by nearly 70 percent after a pro-choice group succeeded in getting the issue on the ballot in November 1998.

These developments are both relevant and important. They are important because in two states ordinary citizens played a vitally important role in the decision-making process on a highly controversial practice. They are also relevant because they show that the existing political processes allow and often challenge Christians to bring their convictions to bear on the pressing social issues of the day.

## Other Recent Cases

### British Columbia, 1993

In British Columbia, Sue Rodriguez, a woman characterized as terminally ill, died by what informed observers now believe was euthanasia. There is no doubt that she underwent the process willingly, for she died shortly after the Supreme Court of Canada narrowly defeated her appeal for the legal right to an assisted death. Svend Robinson, a Member of Parliament from British Columbia who introduced a private member's bill to make assisted suicide legal, was with her when she died. Private member's bills rarely succeed in Canada, but they do succeed in getting the government's attention.

### Saskatchewan, 1995

In Saskatchewan, Robert Latimer received a two-year jail sentence for killing his severely disabled daughter, Tracy. His sentence was confirmed on appeal. However, a year later, a panel of three judges ruled that the original trial judge had erred and that the Canadian Constitution left the courts no alternative but to sentence Latimer to life imprisonment with no chance of parole for at least ten years. In January 2001 the Supreme Court of Canada, in a unanimous 7-0 decision, ruled that Latimer must spend at least ten years in prison for killing his daughter,

12

rejecting the argument that this constituted "cruel and unusual punishment" in Latimer's case.

### Ontario, 1995

Toronto doctor Maurice Genereux received a two-year jail term for assisting two patients in suicide attempts. One attempt failed, and the patient subsequently sued the doctor.

### Nova Scotia, 1995

In Halifax, Nova Scotia, Dr. Nancy Morrison was charged with first-degree murder in the death of a patient with terminal cancer. The case was eventually thrown out of court for lack of evidence that a lethal injection was the actual cause of the patient's death.

### Manitoba, 1998

In Manitoba a judge reversed a local hospital's "do not resuscitate" (DNR) order in the case of a seriously ill patient who had suffered several strokes and was expected to have more. The medical team looking after him considered his quality of life to be so questionable that any effort at resuscitation following another stroke would be pointless. His wife, however, fought the medical determination in court and won a temporary restraining order.

### Ontario, 1999

The *Toronto Star*, Canada's largest newspaper, carried a lead article on the suicide of Marilynne Seguin, a 61-year-old nurse who had been in failing health. The bold headline proclaimed "Death with Dignity," a reference to the Death with Dignity Association Ms. Seguin had founded. Written by noted columnist Tom Harpur, an ordained priest in the Anglican church, the article exuded admiration for this "advocate" of the dying who was reported to have feared "being alive but not living." The greatly admired nurse is said to have counselled more than two thousand patients in their dying.

## Point to Ponder

*Review the cases cited above. Do you believe that in these cases justice was done? What role, if any, should motive have played in sentencing?*

Nearly half of those seeking assisted suicide do so because of extreme mental suffering. Pain-mitigating medicines for mental suffering are more limited than those available for treating physical pain. How should we respond when effective relief is not yet available?

# social factors influencing the discussion

*Scanning the material below will soon reveal that this section paints a grim picture: longer lives, more illnesses, more suffering, more loneliness, more expenses, and more despair. The section ends by predicting legal recognition and social acceptance of compassionate suicide. The message of Synod 2000 is that, from a biblical perspective, those responses would be reprehensible. But what then should a God-honoring, obedient response look like? Suppose that a suffering, elderly believer at the next onset of pneumonia stipulated that no medicine be administered to extend her life—that she receive only painkillers. Death would probably follow soon. . . . The moral choices become much more complex.*

So what do you think? Should this elderly sister's request be honored or should she be treated against her will?

## A Century of Abundant Death

It is remarkable that end-of-life matters became prominent at the close of the twentieth century. Near its beginning, the twentieth century saw the outbreak of war that for the first time encompassed most of the world. Another world war followed, and since then the world has been beset by a long series of regional conflicts. Even today, at the beginning of a new century, many parts of the world still suffer from ethnic, religious, economic, and political wars that undermine and destroy countless lives with unimaginable horror. Starvation stalks much of the developing world, and abortion kills millions of unborn children in North America and elsewhere. Our present discussion is taking place at the end of what was perhaps the most deadly century in the history of the world.

## A Century of Increased Life Expectancy

Paradoxically, the twentieth century was also one of unprecedented breakthroughs in agriculture, medicine, science, technology, and other fields. As a result, there has been a tremendous advance in life-enhancing and life-preserving capabilities. On average, people live longer today than in any previous time.

Ironically, enhanced longevity is posing new challenges of its own.

According to Canadian demographers David Baxter and Andrew Ramlo of Vancouver's Urban Futures Institute, the average life expectancy for both men and women in North America has gone from 49 years in 1901 to 68.5 in 1951 and to 78.4 in 1996. By the year 2021 that number is expected to increase to a life expectancy of around 83 years. Living longer and longer results in very serious consequences. "Baby boomers," the demographers write, "can expect to live long enough to be a problem not only for their children, but their grandchildren and great-grandchildren too" (*Toronto Star,* 12 Aug. 1998).

The Third World faces a reduction in life expectancy. Crippled by debt and epidemics like AIDS, the health care resources of many countries have dwindled to a distressingly low level. Should we ask our government to designate more funds for health care in our nation or should we ask our government to provide more foreign aid to provide better health care in impoverished nations?

The quality of so long a life and the burgeoning cost of health care—at home and in institutions—is beginning to worry many people. As one person said, "Seventy is fine. Ninety sucks. Nobody wants to live that long. You're senile, you're sick, you're in a home. You'd have to be a millionaire to live at a comfortable level that long."

## A Major Shift in Thinking

These new realities, coupled with advances in pharmacology that enable doctors to put patients "to sleep" permanently and without pain, have brought about a marked increase in public receptivity to euthanasia and assisted suicide. That increased receptivity marks a major shift in the way we have traditionally thought about these issues. A number of factors help explain the shift:

### 1. Erosion of Community

Our urban centers have long been experiencing the breakdown of neighborhoods as we once knew them. Often we do not even know our neighbors' names, and we certainly couldn't count on them to look after us when we become frail. Moreover, cultural factors such as consumerism, individualism, careerism, urbanization, and the transient nature of our workforce have greatly contributed to the erosion of a sense of community.

There is evidence in society today that our sense of the value of persons is diminishing and that we may be reaching a point where the elderly, the severely handicapped, and the unborn

16

could be deemed expendable nuisances. Many people cannot even count on their children taking care of them as they age because the children often live too far away.

## 2. Desire for Personal Autonomy

Another factor contributing to the end-of-life discussion is that all over the world there is an increased demand for self-determination, personal autonomy, and individual rights. Until recently, physicians made the key medical decisions for their patients. Doctors expected to do so, and patients assumed they would do so. Today, however, many patients reject medical paternalism. Instead, they embrace the values of informed consent, patients' rights, and death with dignity. A doctor no longer has the final say.

Historically, in North American culture, people tended to defer not only to their doctors but also to God. Life was considered a gift from God, a sacred trust. That perception, too, is shifting. The conviction now is that it's my life and therefore it's my right to decide the how and when of my death, particularly if dying threatens to involve a great deal of suffering and pain.

Which of these positions do you hold? Why?

## 3. Fear of Incremental Death

But often suffering and pain are an inevitable part of the dying process, despite all the care available in our Western world. Many diseases that used to kill randomly across the age groups, such as smallpox and diphtheria, no longer do so. But the diseases associated with long life still do—degenerative diseases like cancer, heart disease, strokes, and dementia. To be sure, the advanced medical skills and technologies of our day are major blessings. They allow us to live better and longer. As the Committee on Medical Ethics of the Episcopal Diocese of Washington puts it, "Today we can draw out a dying process that would have been fairly quick in the past. We have made it possible to die in pieces." Dying in pieces—this is the prospect we dread. This is what fuels our fears: we see ourselves trapped in a prolonged, painful dependency, unable to maintain either dignity or control. The widespread awareness of the possibility of having to experience incremental dying is sufficiently repulsive and terrifying enough for many to consider alternatives.

## 4. Increasing Institutionalization of Death

In our culture the traditional caregivers—mainly women—are now a part of the out-of-home workforce, and so the trend is

Is the institutionalization of infirm and elderly people a good thing? Why or why not?

for people to die in institutions, away from all that's familiar at home. Competent and caring people staff hospitals, nursing homes, and care facilities, and most of them look after their charges very well. But the fact remains that the patients in these institutions find themselves cared for by strangers in environments that are usually much too public. The vital emotional and spiritual needs of these persons at the end of their lives may not be met.

### 5. High Cost of Dying

Medical and technological resources today have a greater capacity than ever before to prolong lives, but these advances are enormously expensive. It is widely known and frequently reported that approximately half of a person's lifelong care cost is spent in the final year of life. In Canada the reductions in federal transfer payments to the provinces have resulted in substantial decreases in many provincial care budgets. Those mostly affected by the cutbacks are usually the sick, the old, and the dying—those who have the weakest voice and the least political clout. When personal finances are depleted and other resources dwindle, patients sometimes come to believe that the *ability* to die turns into the *obligation* to die.

### 6. More Charitable Attitude Toward Compassionate Homicide

So what rights do we really have with regard to our own life and our own death? Are these clear from Scripture?

All the factors mentioned above combine to establish a mood that prompts some to look upon suicide as a possible end-of-life choice. High-profile cases favored by the media make it seem heartless not to grant those suffering people the right to die. And the growing conviction that patients do indeed have rights regarding their own deaths increasingly removes the moral taboos that used to serve as barriers. Together all of these conditions lend force to the demand for legal recognition and social acceptance of compassionate homicide.

## Point to Ponder

*A small group discussed the challenge of caring for elderly parents. One member read from 1 Timothy 5:8: "If anyone does not provide for his relatives, and especially for his immediate family, he has denied the faith and is worse than an unbeliever." He wondered whether that would mean that the Bible demanded that he take in his aging parent.*

*Someone countered that was probably not the case. In Paul's day people hardly ever reached an age much beyond fifty. He added that today's elderly demand nearly around-the-clock care. Some people in their seventies may still have an older mother. What do you think? How should we apply that text to our own aging relatives?*

# biblical foundations for how christians should regard end-of-life issues

*An essential point in our discussion of end-of-life issues is to determine what God's will is, because God is the author, owner, and sustainer of human life. So at this point the report turns to an examination of what God's Word teaches us about these matters.*

## God's Gift of Life

"I am not my own, but belong, body and soul, in life and in death, to my faithful Savior, Jesus Christ" (Heidelberg Catechism, Q&A 1). This confession encapsulates the core belief of members of the Christian Reformed Church. The way we view life and, consequently, how we approach death should reflect our absolute trust in our faithful Lord and Savior. We must look to God's Word for our understanding of the meaning of life and death.

From the very beginning that Word makes clear that life is a special and unique gift. Both humankind and animals are referred to in Genesis as "living beings," but only of humankind is it said that God "breathed into his nostrils the breath of life" (Gen. 2:7). There is something warmly personal and intimate in this picture. God did not just give life; he gave something of himself—as Jesus did when he "breathed on" his disciples and gave them the Holy Spirit (John 20:22).

As a part of creation reflecting the very image of God (Gen. 1:26-27), each person has inestimable worth as an individual and as a member of a community. Recognizing God's image in self and others means respecting and cherishing the creativity, compassion, love for life, and longing for community with which we are created.

Does this mean that human life is of ultimate value? Are there conditions under which human life should be endangered or even willingly taken?

God's intention for human life is well expressed by the Westminster Catechism: "What is the chief purpose of man? To know God and enjoy Him forever" (Q&A 1). We can broaden the scope of this confession to include the enjoyment of God, others, self, and the creation.

Yet, though life is clearly God's gift to us, it is a gift more of stewardship than of ownership. We are called to be caretakers of all that has been given to us. We are free to live our lives as fully as we can, but our freedom remains limited by our responsibility to be faithful to God. And there are values beyond that of life. Our love for God and others sometimes should take precedence over our own lives. This is the kind of love Jesus demonstrated in his willingness to lay down his life for us.

With the gift of life comes the responsibility to use it wisely. God commands us to protect life and not to take it into our own hands. He will require an accounting for every human life, "for in the image of God has God made man" (Gen. 9:5-6). In the Sermon on the Mount, Jesus reaffirmed the commandment not to kill, replacing the desire to hurt with the requirement to love and care for one's neighbor and even one's enemy (Matt. 5:21-22, 43-44). Then he went on to instruct his followers in the law that fulfills the prohibition against murder, the positive command to love and be reconciled to one another. Paul summarizes that teaching of our Lord in Romans 13:9-10: "The commandments, 'Do not commit adultery,' 'Do not murder,' 'Do not steal,' 'Do not covet,' and whatever other commandment there may be, are summed up in this one rule: 'Love your neighbor as yourself.' Love does no harm to its neighbor. Therefore love is the fulfillment of the law."

Jesus affirmed the value of life by participating fully in our life on earth. Yet he did not hesitate to sacrifice himself and to make his life an offering to the Father: "Here I am, I have come to do your will" (Heb. 10:9). He teaches that the real value of life lies not in how much we cling to it but rather under what circumstances we are willing to lay it down: "For whoever wants to save his life will lose it, but whoever loses his life for me and for the gospel will save it" (Mark 8:35).

## The Bible and Suicide

In view of the growing demand for the legalization of assisted suicide, an examination of biblical givens may be helpful. The call to be willing to lose one's life in order to save it is mentioned six times in the four gospels (Matt. 10:39; Mark 8:35; Luke 9:24; 14:26-27; 17:33; John 12:25). These words of our Lord have prompted many acts of courage and compassion in which individuals were willing to sacrifice their own lives in order to serve others in his name. But such selfless acts of sacrificial love and compassion are not to be confused with the conditions that lead a person to attempt suicide.

Interestingly, the instances of suicide that are mentioned in the Bible do not include explicit condemnation of the act (see 2 Sam. 1:24-25; 2:4-7; also 17:23; Judg. 9:52-54; 1 Kings 16:18-19; Matt. 27:5). However, this must not be taken to mean that the Bible condones suicide. Scripture clearly prohibits all wanton destruction of human life, and that includes the willful ending of one's own life. The Heidelberg Catechism affirms this when it says, in its treatment of the sixth commandment, "I am not to harm or recklessly endanger myself either."

Although the scriptural narratives referred to do not explicitly condemn those who took their own lives, their desperate actions *are* generally associated with lives of disobedience. Again, however, these examples of suicide must not be understood to suggest that depressed or suicidal persons today have, at some point in their lives, chosen to pursue the way of evil. We now know that depression is a very serious illness, one that can have fatal consequences. It is of special comfort, therefore, for believers to know that, although the Bible does not condone suicide, our gracious God is certainly able to forgive it.

## The Church's Attitude Toward Suicide

In the early church, Christians (such as Paul) viewed their own acceptance of suffering and death as a sharing in or even a completion of Christ's suffering (Col. 1:24; 2 Cor. 1:5). The early church honored martyrdom but stressed doing all one could—short of betraying one's faith—to avoid it.

Saint Augustine in *The City of God* (fourth century A.D.) offered a systematic argument against suicide, a position based on the beliefs and attitudes of his predecessors. His arguments were based on the classical virtues and on common sense rather than on biblical evidence. His goal was to oppose those who encouraged suicide as an ultimate act of piety.

Augustine's argument led to a strong condemnation of suicide in the medieval church. In the thirteenth century Thomas

Passive euthanasia usually refers to the absence of aggressive medical treatment for a patient who is terminally ill. Active euthanasia usually refers to situations in which medical intervention, such as a lethal injection, causes the onset of death and is performed with an eye toward shortening life. Is that a helpful distinction? Why or why not?

Suicide has assumed alarming dimensions. Some thirty thousand cases were reported in the United States in 1996. Among them are Christians. Would you agree with the following assertions? God judges none of them for the deed of suicide itself but whether they are in Christ. Mental anguish can be so excruciatingly painful that even believers are driven to end their own lives. They are ushered into the presence of God like all other sinners saved by grace. (In debating these questions please be very sensitive to those in your group whose loved ones may have ended their own lives.)

Aquinas argued that shortening one's life is wrong not only because it violates the commandment against murder but also because it is a sin against the God who is the giver of life. Moreover, he felt that suicide cut short the time for a person to repent. The medieval church took a strong stand against it. The church of that day condemned all those who had taken their own lives, even in the name of piety, and denied them a Christian burial.

How would you evaluate the argument that suicide cannot be forgiven by God because the person committing this deed cannot repent of it or ask God for forgiveness?

Increasingly in the twentieth century many Christians have tempered their attitude on this issue. They recognize that persons caught up in despair are often so burdened by life that suicide seems the only solution. Today the church seeks to offer hope to suicidal persons and to bring comfort to those who are left behind in grief after a suicide.

## Point to Ponder

*John B. Burgers, a Presbyterian theologian, points out that Christ's excruciating pain, especially during the last hours on the cross, had supreme redemptive value. He then suggests that the suffering of believers in Christ has "redemptive possibilities":*

> *In the experience of pain, both physical and psychological, believers draw on the deepest resources of faith and grace. Believers around them share in that experience each in their own way. On the one hand Christians will, together with all people of good will, seek to mitigate pain and suffering, and they will endeavor to eliminate conditions that cause suffering in society, but on the other hand they recognize that pain can be a matter of meaning, an occasion for the sufferer to search for meaning, consolation and the strength of Christ. The Christian community around the sufferer will interpret this spiritual process for itself and be the richer for it.*

—*Theology Today,* Vol. 51, No. 2, July 1994, pp. 204-218

*Consider some instances in your own life or in the life of someone you know where this has indeed been the case.*

# when the gift of life becomes a burden

*This section of the report explores the biblical command to relieve suffering and to show mercy to those in need. But how far should we take this? How do we balance the values of relieving suffering and protecting human life when these two values conflict?*

The gift of life can indeed become a burden. Our most appropriate response to suffering is compassion, reaching out in love to individuals in a time of need. Our compassion signals that we want to help and to do all that is possible to alleviate their distress. Compassion compels us to ease pain and suffering. Not to do so is wrong.

As Christians we have a fundamental obligation to do all we can—short of acting with the intention to kill—to relieve pain and suffering. We therefore cannot simply dismiss the pain of others because it may have a redemptive aspect. And we certainly may not impose suffering on others. God does not desire his people to suffer. For all who do suffer, he promises, "I will turn their mourning into gladness; I will give them comfort and joy instead of sorrow" (Jer. 31:13).

Should we authorize pain relief for a distressed dying person if we know that doing so might shorten her life?

Nevertheless, God's Word teaches us that some aspects of suffering *can* be redemptive. In writing to the Colossians, Paul indicates his willingness to share in the suffering of the saints, seeing in it a sharing in the living sacrifice offered on our behalf by our Lord (Col. 1:24). The apostle Peter affirms a faith that is proved genuine through "grief in all kinds of trials" (1 Pet. 1:6). And the psalmist says, "It was good for me to be afflicted so that I might learn your decrees" (Ps. 119:71).

But suffering is not always redemptive in Scripture. Job's despair in the depths of his suffering requires a better response than his wordy friends offer him. Their compassionate silence as they sit with him for seven days and seven nights to "sympathize with him and comfort him" (Job 2:11) may have been

23

In 1 Peter 4:12-13 we read, "Dear friends, do not be surprised at the painful trial you are suffering, as though something strange were happening to you. But rejoice that you participate in the sufferings of Christ, so that you may be overjoyed when his glory is revealed." Could you conceive of these verses as a source of consolation for a suffering person? Would these words have some bearing on the issue of euthanasia?

How can the church community "link hands with the suffering and dying?"

Share some concrete examples of times in your own life when someone has helped you carry a burden.

more valuable than all their words. David cried out to God, "My God, my God, why have you forsaken me?" (Ps. 22:1), words that our Lord himself cries from the cross. Christ's prayer to let the cup pass from him in the Garden of Gethsemane reflects his own struggle in accepting the hell he faced in his death.

## Carrying Each Other's Burdens

Motivated by God's own compassion for hurting people, we must not allow those who suffer to bear the burden alone. We must take seriously our unity in the body of Christ. The Christian moral values we affirm in family, church, and community do not apply only in personal attitudes and intentions; they also have a social dimension. The church community is a community that shares burdens and that links hands with the suffering and the dying.

On the other hand, a sense of being forsaken by one's fellow believers adds enormously to suffering. The feeling of loneliness becomes especially acute at this point in our lives. Here we face a great challenge today because most of us are reluctant to take on end-of-life care for others. As Dr. Hessel Bouma III put it in a speech at Calvin College (15 Jan. 1997), "Ask people where they would prefer to die, and 80 percent indicate they would prefer to die at home, surrounded by family and friends. Ask these same people whether they'd be willing to care for someone who is dying in his or her home, and a similar majority responds, No. What we desire for ourselves, we're reluctant to offer to others."

Paul urges the Galatians to care for one another: "Carry each other's burdens, and in this way you will fulfill the law of Christ" (Gal. 6:2). But he also recognizes that "each one should carry his own load" (Gal. 6:5). In southern India, where many women still traditionally carry heavy loads on their heads, shoulder-high stone platforms are placed at regular intervals along the roadways. These platforms are called "burden bearers." When the women come to one of these stone shelves, they can set their load down and rest under the shade of a nearby tree. They are not relieved of their load, but, after a period of rest, they have been energized enough to take up their burden again. Ultimately our brothers and sisters who struggle with the burden of a hard and painful death must deal with that burden themselves. However, when the Christian community surrounds them in love, that burden is temporarily lifted. They experience rest and renewed strength so that they can again "carry their own load," as Paul said.

## Point to Ponder

*Dr. L. S. Baer describes how, as a young physician thirty years ago, he saved the life of 81-year-old Mrs. Stone, who was bedridden, in constant pain, and of a failing mind. When she had a heart attack, he and a medical team at the hospital applied all the medical know-how of their day and saved the patient. She lived for just under two years in a home, unable to see and hear much, helpless and incontinent. Looking back, Dr. Baer writes: "This case is typical of what is still routinely done to thousands of older patients in this country with the best of intentions. But far too often we ward off death and in the process kill living. Just thirty years before that event, nothing could have been done for Mrs. Stone, and she would have mercifully died. Today, thirty years after the event, we are faced with medical and technical measures one hundred times as effective."*

—Let the Patient Decide: A Doctor's Advice to Older Persons,
Louis Shattuck Baer, M.D., Philadelphia: The Westminster Press, 1989.

*Should Dr. Baer have saved this patient? Who should decide on the course of treatment? The patient? The doctor? The family?*

# four vignettes

*In this session you'll find lots of reading. If you're using this report in a discussion setting it would be best if participants come prepared, having read these stories at home. If they have not, be sure to take ample time to do so now, because your discussion will focus specifically on these stories. Even if your group has read these vignettes at home, be sure to refresh your collective memory by briefly reviewing the major contours of each story before launching your discussion.*

We turn now to vignettes illustrating how people and their communities responded when the gift of life became a burden.

## The Latimer Case

The story of Tracy Latimer has held the attention of the Canadian public for over six years. Although this is not a story of a person nearing the end of her life, it does illustrate a number of issues relevant to the thrust of this report. Specifically, the case is included because it involves the dilemmas faced by judicial law, the significance of public opinion in determining the application of the law, the importance of a pain-management plan, and the issue of mercy killing.

On Sunday, October 24, 1993, Robert Latimer of Battleford, Saskatchewan, quietly picked up his twelve-year old daughter, Tracy, carried her into his pickup truck, and ran the engine until his daughter fell into a carbon monoxide-induced sleep. His wife and other children returned from a church service to find Tracy lying dead in her bed. Soon after, Mr. Latimer called the local police to report that Tracy had died in her sleep. An autopsy revealed high levels of carbon monoxide, and Mr. Latimer was subsequently taken into custody and charged with second-degree murder.

Tracy Latimer had had a severe case of cerebral palsy since birth, when she was deprived of oxygen. She had never developed beyond the mental level of a three-year-old, could not talk or walk, and was incontinent. She was virtually immobile, could move only her head and one arm, and was bedridden. Differing opinions exist as to whether or not her pain was bearable. Experts at Mr. Latimer's trial testified that her pain could have been relieved through medication and surgery. But surgeons and some caregivers testified that she was in constant pain. Yet her mother's journal cited days when Tracy was happy, alert, and cheerful.

Tracy had endured a series of painful operations. She was unable to take painkillers while recovering from surgery because those drugs would worsen her eating, breathing, and digestive problems. An orthopedic surgeon testified that Tracy was in extreme pain in the days before her death and that her future would have involved incredible suffering from further operations. Just days before her death, her family had been informed that yet another surgery would be required to remove a thighbone that was causing intense pain.

The public discussion that surrounded court judgments and appeals showed a surprising amount of sympathy for Mr. Latimer. The court itself seesawed back and forth about his sentence—from a slap on the wrist (two years on parole) to ten years without parole. Justice Noble, who presided over one of the appeals, granted Latimer a constitutional exemption (which was successfully appealed in 1998) from the minimum ten-year sentence on the basis that this sentence would constitute "cruel and unusual punishment," forbidden in the Canadian Charter of Rights and Freedoms. "Latimer is not a threat to society," he explained. He further commented that this act of homicide was "committed for caring and altruistic reasons."

There was no suggestion by any witness that Latimer killed his daughter because she was disabled, only that he did so to end the pain that accompanied her illness. Evidence showed that Latimer was motivated solely by his love and compassion for his daughter, by the desire to end her suffering. As Justice Noble stated,

> It is admittedly a difficult task to prove what motivated a person to carry out such a grave act as murder that was not somehow related to self-interest, malevolence, hate or violence. But in my view of the evidence presented in this case, which is for the most part clear and uncontradicted, we have that rare act of homicide that was committed for

caring and altruistic reasons. That is why it is, for want of a better term, sometimes called "compassionate homicide."

In sentencing Latimer the judge said

> While you wrongly took her life you appeared to do so for compassionate and not malevolent or selfish reasons. . . . But having said that, I must say to you that murder, no matter what the circumstances that bring it about, will never be as a matter of law a forgivable offense. The stigma that attaches to an act of murder is, in the eyes of right-minded people, as grave as it gets under our system of justice. I recognize that you must live with that stigma for the rest of your life. In your case it is clear . . . that you acted altruistically, but you nevertheless took the life of a human being and you did so deliberately.

The general public, with the exception of groups representing the disabled community, appeared to sympathize more strongly with Latimer than with his daughter. Even some church groups supported his action. The public judged Latimer's action in much the same way it would judge putting an animal out of its pain.

Organizations representing the disabled, however, have disputed the claim that Latimer ended Tracy's life because of pain and not because she was disabled. They have argued that no father would have done this to a healthy, exuberant adolescent without incurring the outrage of the public. The disabled fear that the value of their lives has been placed into question by the lenient sentence of the court as well as by public sentiment condoning this "compassionate act of homicide," an expression that, to them, is a contradiction in terms.

In January 2001, advocates for the disabled were relieved when the Supreme Court of Canada ruled that Latimer must serve at least ten years in prison.

Tracy Latimer's medical plight illustrates an additional issue. Had it not been for medical technology she would probably not have survived her early childhood. Modern medicine lengthened her life, thus prolonging her suffering. Tracy's situation may also have been such that modern painkillers did not fully mitigate her pain and suffering. Would you call the father's action murder? Would he deserve a murderer's sentence?

## Nigel Martin's story

The story of Nigel Martin's place in his church, his family, and his school is included in this report because it shows the significance of a supporting community in coping with tragedy, the essence of Christian compassion, the power of practical assistance in the church community, and the power of the disabled to make us "see."

For Brian and Evelyn Martin it was a robbery in the night. On the night of October 10, 1985, sudden-infant-death syndrome (SIDS) robbed their youngest son, Nigel, of the full and rich life they anticipated for him. Nigel did survive the robbery, but it deprived him of almost all conscious functioning. When two months later the Martins finally took him home from the hospital, he was very different from the robust, bright-eyed boy he had been. It was a time "clouded by fearful anxiety," wrote Brian. "Evelyn and I felt truly alone. Nigel was unresponsive, unsmiling and seemingly unaware of his environment." Responses to family and friends were so subtle that a casual observer would not detect them.

The fourteen years since Nigel's SIDS experience have been filled with hospitalizations, bouts with pneumonia, endless appointments with medical doctors and care workers, long and tedious tube feedings, suctioning, ventilator treatments, intense chest physiotherapy, and exercising of limbs. Nevertheless, despite all these efforts, Nigel has had to suffer rigidity; contractions of the hands, feet, spine, and hips; and painful hip surgery to support a progressive spinal curvature.

Today Nigel is a teenager who cannot walk, speak, swallow, hear, or see, and he has no obvious way of communicating with anyone. "When Nigel's symptoms were initially recited," says Brian, "they became a litany of despair that seemed to avoid the central issue—that he was a child."

Over the years the Martins have developed strong connections to other families who have experienced similar circumstances. Gradually their thinking shifted from the trauma they had experienced to an appreciation of this new person their son had become. "The problems Nigel faced had not disappeared," says Brian, "but the perceptions of these problems which were preventing us from seeing our son had."

In networking with people who had similar needs, the Martins experienced the profound meaning of grace and compassion. People at Fellowship Christian Reformed Church (Edmonton, Alberta), where the Martins are members, freely offered practical assistance. They provided child care, occasionally took the other Martin children to movies or sports events, or drove them to their music lessons. Others prepared and delivered meals. Some people with nursing experience occasionally looked after Nigel for an evening or a few days to give Evelyn and Brian some rest. Some assisted with the vigorous patterning exercises Nigel needed to go through. And people prayed, individually and collectively, for healing and support.

Today Nigel's' presence at Edmonton Christian Junior High School is accepted by the students as quite natural. A classmate on the way to gym class will grab his wheelchair. "I'll push him," he volunteers. Friends linger near his wheelchair during his tube feeding and ask, "Is Nigel coming outside?" A too exuberant classmate may jostle him, resulting in Nigel's letting out a sonorous howl and jolting up his arms and stiffening his body. As Nigel relaxes again, another classmate may pick up his cloth from the floor and tenderly place it under Nigel's chin. Other students push him on the skating rink, clamoring for their turn to push his chair. "Even though you can't talk, I still think you are a nice boy," writes one classmate. Another writes, "I think you are cool," and another. "You are fun to play with and to talk to, and you never tell a secret."

In light of the extent of Nigel's disabilities, it is nothing less than astonishing to see how thoroughly his family and his peers have included Nigel in their lives. "We have felt grace in the little things," Evelyn and Brian state. They mention birthday parties that Nigel has been invited to and the way caring parents have attended to details so that Nigel can be a part of the celebrations. They are thankful for the gift of hospitality that God has given. Evelyn and Brian count on just such a gift to hold the future for Nigel.

The future is something the Martins think about frequently. Long ago they stopped thinking back on the person Nigel was before his SIDS incident. They hope some day their son will have an identity apart from them, will be an independent person in his own right, treated with dignity and respect, with a valued place within the Christian community and the broader society. They testify to the presence of God's grace in their own and Nigel's lives, and they continue to rely on the constancy of God's love to uphold them and Nigel. They believe that God will renew their strength, that God's love and faithfulness are large enough to fill their own and Nigel's needs.

That hope is perhaps most poignantly illustrated in a set of two-panel banners designed by Evelyn and titled "Dreams of Heaven I" and "Dreams of Heaven II." In the first panel Nigel, in his wheelchair, is represented as entering a kind of pathway. As he moves into and along it, he is slowly transformed into a leaping, walking boy. This panel represents the dream that was the prayer of the Martins and their community when Nigel first returned home as a totally changed boy. In the second panel Nigel doesn't change at all; instead, as he enters the pathway, it is the people around him who change. A spiritual revolution takes place as Nigel is totally loved and completely accepted for who he is, surrounded by his community. And he is still in his chair, still the same person.

Nigel's presence in the community makes a difference to those around him. "It is you, Nigel," wrote Brian, "who teach us . . . you have patiently endured our sadness, our mistakes, our giving up and coming back again. You sit peacefully. Like the lily of the field or the birds of the air, neither do you toil or spin. . . ."

## A Clinical Vignette

Dr. Lawrence Feenstra, a medical practitioner in Grand Rapids, Michigan, contributed the following account. We include this story because it is an example of a physician's caring relationship with an elderly couple over many years. It illustrates the variety of support services that combined to bring this couple spiritual and physical comfort, and it includes a sample of a care directive both husband and wife completed in consultation with their family. The words are those of Dr. Feenstra.

An armed forces chaplain and his wife retired to western Michigan in 1980 and became my patients for the next fifteen years. Both individuals suffered from significant ongoing medical problems that required regular medical care. He had medical mellius, mild hypertension, and a prior myocardial infarction, which led to cardiac surgery. She had a history of cardiac rhythm disturbance, hypothyroidism, and a lung condition (sarcoidosis) which caused coughing and shortness of breath. Their fifteen years of regular office visits developed into the meaningful patient-physician relationships that are so valued in the field of internal medicine.

In the mid-1980s the wife developed weakness in her left hand. Over the next three years similar weakness developed insidiously in the right upper extremity and eventually the legs as well. A diagnosis of amyotropic lateral sclerosis (ALS), or Lou Gehrig's disease, was made, and over the subsequent seven to eight years gradually increasing disability affected ambulation, the simple tasks of self-care, swallowing, and speech so that she required increasing assistance from her husband and

Review the various forms of Christian service in the Nigel Martin account. In many cases of prolonged suffering the community rallies with loving support. And unsuspected blessings become apparent. Would you say that Nigel's suffering and that of his parents found some meaning in the outpouring of love of their friends?

family. This support was always provided and was instrumental in avoiding serious respiratory infections. She remained alert, able to communicate, and without physical discomfort. Activity inside and outside the home was gradually decreased, but it was maintained by an attentive family until it was no longer possible.

In 1992 the family was devastated when the husband was diagnosed with prostate cancer, which, despite radical surgery, irradiation, hormonal and chemotherapy, proved to be an aggressive form of neoplasm. Within one year it had spread to the spine and pelvis, leading to progressively severe bone pain, which necessitated vigorous and increasingly aggressive pain control.

Since the husband had always functioned very effectively as the wife's primary caregiver, his own health problems now led to increased family involvement as well as to ongoing care from many friends and their entire church family. During this period a new granddaughter (their first) proved to be a blessing that enriched their lives despite the ongoing pain and disabilities.

In 1991 both the husband and the wife, after discussion together and with their family, completed a Designation of Patient Advocate Form, a form commonly used in the state of Michigan, which includes directions for health care and durable power of attorney. Specifically, the form states,

> I do not want my life to be prolonged by providing or continuing life-sustaining treatment if any of the following medical conditions exist:
>
> 1. I am in an irreversible coma or persistent vegetative state.
>
> 2. I am terminally ill and life-sustaining procedures would serve only to artificially delay my death.
>
> 3. Under any circumstances where my medical condition is such that the burdens of treatment outweigh the benefits, I want my patient advocate to consider the relief of suffering and the quality of my life as well as the extent of possibly prolonging my life. I understand that this decision could or would allow me to die.

Ultimately we cannot fathom the why of suffering and pain. Why would a godly couple such as the chaplain and his wife have to traverse such a deep valley? Still, by faith, we conclude that, in the company of Jesus, they came out of that suffering victoriously. The army chaplain and his wife testified to that all along to their friends. In their case "redemptive possibilities" became glorious realities! Still, some of us might feel uneasy about some of the wording of the Designation of Patient Advocate Form they filled out. Do you believe the terms of this directive were appropriate for them? Are they appropriate for those you love? For you?

33

The final year of life for this couple, in addition to the ongoing caring support of family, friends, and almost their entire church, was characterized also by the outstanding contributions of a local hospice organization, which all together rendered harmonious, caring attention to spiritual and physical comfort.

The husband died peacefully at home in 1995. His wife remained at home under hospice and family care and also died peacefully, less than six months later.

## Beth Mohr's story

This story has been included in our report because it illustrates some difficult choices between the saving of the life of a mother or that of her baby, an example of a person facing death and preparing for it, the necessity of a good hospice program, and a shining example of the communion of the saints.

Beth Lynn (De Bruyne) Mohr, wife of family physician Jeffrey Mohr and mother of David, Jonathan, and Benjamin, died in her Hudsonville, Michigan, home in the early morning hours of June 15, 1998, following a three-year struggle with brain cancer. She was 35 years old.

In September of 1995, when Beth was thirty-four weeks pregnant, she was diagnosed with a malignant brain tumor. The Mohrs knew about tumors. Beth was a nurse trained in oncology (the study of tumors), and Jeff's own medical training had left him no stranger to the devastation such growths usually cause. When they received the test results, the implications were immediately clear. Left untreated, Beth's cancer would prove fatal within a year.

Because brain cancer does not normally spread to other parts of the body, it posed no immediate danger to the baby. The indicated treatment, however, was a different story. Chemotherapy affects the bloodstream and could harm the baby, and surgical intervention could cause fetal distress.

Beth had always been annoyed with the way people, even medical people, avoided discussion about end-of-life matters. Although death is an inescapable fact of life, it is generally not talked about. But while avoiding this critical issue may be a universal strategy, it was not Beth's way. And so, having explored all the difficult options together and their implications for the baby, Beth decided with Jeff to undergo surgery immediately. Realizing that complications in the surgery could be fatal for Beth, together she and Jeff decided to have the medical team take the baby by C-section if at any time during the operation the fetus should be in danger.

Fortunately, the surgery had no ill effect on the baby. It did, however, reveal a tumor of a kind and size that indicated a maximum survival time of six months for Beth. It was thus a matter of great urgency for the baby to be delivered so that Beth could receive the treatment indicated. Beth started taking steroids to stimulate the baby's lung maturity and advance the time of its external viability. On October 3, 1995, a healthy Benjamin Lynn was delivered by C-section.

Following Ben's birth, Beth initially responded well to extensive radiation and chemotherapy treatments. God gave her and Jeff another year of grace and good times, during which Beth lived a fairly normal life, even driving a car. But her ability to organize things was deteriorating, her short-term memory was affected, and one of her legs started giving her difficulty in walking.

In the fall of 1997 another scan showed a new tumor and renewed activity of the first one. Beth decided, with Jeff, to forgo further aggressive treatment and to enter a hospice program at home. In retrospect, Jeff felt that once this decision was made, Beth almost looked forward to receiving hospice care. She knew she was dying, and she wanted to die in the trusted surroundings of her home.

Not many people know a great deal about hospice programs. As Jeff put it, "Our culture lags behind the hospice movement. Society feels that accepting hospice care means giving up, that it's a quitting of the fight to maintain life." For Beth and Jeff it meant no such thing. For them it meant having comforting space and precious time to prepare for the inevitable end and to do so with the caring support of relatives, friends, and specially trained persons.

Patients entering hospice care are not expected to live longer than six months. A medical doctor has to prepare a certificate to that effect before a patient can be admitted. Hospice care is therefore not appropriate for all terminally ill patients, but it was for Beth, even though, as it turned out, she was in hospice care for two months beyond the normally anticipated duration.

Beth remained at home, surrounded by her family. A hospice nurse helped out up to two hours a day, five days a week. It was especially in the course of those eight months that Beth and Jeff learned how great a comfort the active care and support of family, friends, and the church community can be. They also discovered how complex such care often is and how much careful planning and organizing it involves.

A large room in the house became Beth's room. Jeff also slept there, and the boys at times took turns looking after their mom at night. Jeff believes that the boys were themselves comforted in being with Beth. But as her nights became more and more restless, Beth needed the type of constant, ongoing attention Jeff and the boys could not provide alone. That is when relatives, friends, and members of their church, Orchard Hill Reformed Church in Grand Rapids, began to sit with her, allowing Jeff the occasional respite he needed. In her last week on earth, Beth's parents moved into the house. Beth died early in the morning hours of June 15, 1998, surrounded by those who loved her most dearly.

For the better part of a year, up to and even after Beth died, the support the Mohrs received from the community was extraordinary. Essentials such as meals, dishes, laundry, and the many other household chores that form part of the day-to-day living of a family of five were all taken care of. Jeff's church, for example, prepared meals three times a week. Neighbors and relatives looked after nearly everything the other days.

Beth's father, a gifted organizer who arranged the sit-ins, managed the sleepovers, and scheduled the preparation and delivery of all the meals, described some of the reactions of the caregivers. One said, "I wanted to be able to minister to those who had ministered to us in so many ways." Another observed, "I knew that helping care for Beth in her home allowed her to die with peace and dignity. I could not change the fact that Beth was dying, but I could make her last few months more meaningful to her and her family."

Beth's father also reflected on a very special event—the healing service that was held for Beth. Scripture reading, prayers, and the laying on of hands by the many people present had a profound impact on Beth and all those present. God did not see fit to heal her physically, but, as her father reported, her soul and spirit were touched, as everyone else in that service was.

Often, as individuals were thanked for their help, their response was to thank the family for letting them be involved. As one person put it, "I cannot even begin to explain what I received from this experience. Not only did I do more than I thought possible, but it opened my thoughts to my own future. It created a bond between me and the family that cannot be explained." Another one said, "These times were so precious. Being able to pray for her and the family in her presence during the night was such a blessing. By morning I felt that I had had a deep spiritual experience."

Jeff Mohr is hugely thankful for the many ways in which his community was "there" for Beth, for him, and for the boys. No one should underestimate the heavy and multidimensional burden that comes with the dying of a loved one, nor the degree to which it can be shared and, in the sharing, be made more bearable through the care that a loving community can provide.

In the spring of 1998 there was an outpouring of love in grief that gave rich meaning to the expression "communion of the saints" in the Michigan town of Hudsonville.

## Point to Ponder
*What can we do individually and communally for neighbors, acquaintances, and associates who face end-of-life challenges without the support of a church community? Do we know where to begin? How can we find out?*

The accounts of a church community providing such a variety of services are heartwarming. It shows that the blessed use of the spiritual and physical resource of communities can work miracles! It also shows how important it is for people to belong to communities of this type. It is a tragedy that so many people around the world have no community. Evaluate your church's ability to minister in this way. Would you be sufficiently confident of your church's support if you were faced with the same decision as Beth and Jeff?

# toward communities of care

*What can and should we do for those who are dying? What part can the church play in meeting the needs of those who are nearing the end of their lives? The report here presents a strong challenge to faith communities to serve as the hands and heart of our Great Physician.*

What accounts for the very different outcomes of the four cases described in section five? No doubt the personal weaknesses, strengths, and resources of the different families. But it was also the network of their caregivers, friends, and church community that made the difference. The resources of a community of care made the difference between capitulation and persistence. Those resources can make the difference in the end-of-life experience.

Taking effective steps toward the practice of community is our challenge. Our society's individualism severely handicaps the practice of community. Far too many people have virtually no network of support. Even within a caring community, few of us can provide ideal conditions for chronic or palliative care. But with the help of even imperfect support networks, we can make a blessed difference. All of us can take small steps, and each step helps. After all, if we say that life is so precious that we may not end it, we must give every life a valid—and valued—place in the community. Out of the myriad of ways we can be there for each other, we mention the following.

The word *palliative* comes from the Latin *palliatus* which means "cloaked," "muffled." The care given to the patient is no longer focused on healing but on alleviating discomfort and pain. Do you agree that there comes a point when the focus of treatment should turn from extending life to improving the quality of what is left of it?

## Providing Pastoral Care

We begin with pastoral care simply because that is what we expect from the church community, and few persons are better equipped to minister to the chronically ill and dying and their families than their pastors and fellow believers. Pastors work with the themes of hope and forgiveness, purpose, assurance, and comfort.

The imminence of death has a way of breaking down the walls that often block pastoral ministry. Healthy people sometimes keep their faith separate from their life issues, but when death encroaches, faith and life become inextricably connected.

As death approaches, pastoral workers play various key roles. Approaching death raises theological questions. Even though few of these will be phrased in theological language, sensitive pastors and fellow believers will recognize and articulate them. At such a time they can help clarify relationships, particularly the all-important ultimate relationships. Sensitive pastors and fellow members also know the power of empathetic listening. They know that entering into the dying person's story validates that person's life, affirms connections with the larger world, and acknowledges that he or she has made a difference. As they lead members to God's throne in prayer, serve them communion, or sing with them, those who provide pastoral care affirm a bond that's comforting and precious, a bond not merely between friends on earth but also between friends of God. As they move from the bedside of the dying to the working and worshiping community, pastoral workers may, as we shall see, pass on some of their pastoral skills and insights to their parishioners and help mobilize them for ministry.

## Facing the Need for Inclusion

Illness is isolating, and the sense of isolation is heightened for those who suffer chronic and terminal illness in institutional settings away from home. This is why we favor the home-care option and hospice care wherever that is desired and can be afforded or arranged. The home, after all, is the place where the patient is surrounded by all that is loved and familiar. It breathes security. True, friends may continue to drop by without realizing that their visits may intrude on badly needed privacy, but their attention shows that they continue to care. Home is also the place where the family has talked and sung and prayed together. That too continues. Are there sensitive, even intimate issues to resolve? Dad's anger? Mom's fear of what's ahead? Home is the place to talk about these things, especially in the face of death.

But often it is just not possible to take care of our dying loved ones at home. When hospitals and nursing homes are the only choice, it is even more important that we include the sick and dying in our lives. When they visit, hospital chaplains, pastors, relatives, and fellow believers link the dying person to the body of believers and to God. So does the inclusion of the dying in announcements and in prayers. But we must go beyond a superficial mention that "Julie Best is still at Memorial Hospital." The congregation needs to know how to pray for Julie, what to ask for, and how they can help her and her family in specific ways. Friends who wish to visit may need to be advised to call ahead and keep their visits brief. They may be encouraged to send a card or a note. Some friends may be reluctant to visit, afraid that they won't know what to say. But listening is also a gift, and "90 percent of caring is just showing up." Pastors should encourage members of their congregations to develop their skills of listening and caring.

## Easing the Fear of Dying

Though most people fear death, believers can conquer that fear. God's grace is capable of giving believers a wonderful assurance of faith. Still, not all believers reach that point, and even those who do rarely attain it without struggle. We fear death, after all, because it is the end of life as we know it, and we cannot see what's on the other side. Many Christians experience the conflicting elements of the process of dying—depression, denial, anger, bargaining, acceptance, and hope.

Appropriate ministry to the dying offers them the freedom to acknowledge these doubts and fears. Scripture itself, as in Psalm 88, acknowledges these realities. As we identify with fellow believers, we point them to the gospel, to hope, and to freedom from fear. We remind each other of the fact that nothing, neither life nor death, shall separate us from the love of God. We rest in Christ's atoning work for us, and we take hold of the promise of life everlasting and the resurrection of the dead. We work with the Scriptures, which remind us of these certainties, and we lead each other close to God in prayer. And when fears and doubt linger, we keep on pointing each other to the one whom the Scriptures say is "greater than our hearts, and he knows everything" (1 John 3:20). In this hope we lead each other to the comforting conviction that even though we "walk through the valley of the shadow of death, [we] will fear no evil" (Ps. 23:4).

## Managing Pain and Suffering

Earlier we noted that pain and the fear of pain and of death itself play a huge role in creating a climate of sympathy for assisted suicide and euthanasia. Yet, contrary to popular belief, studies show that people who actually experience severe pain are not more likely than others to favor ending their lives. As

41

the Episcopal Diocesan Committee on Medical Ethics explains, "Patients are interested in getting rid of their pain—not in ending their lives" (p. 53).

But there is disagreement on whether patients who have severe pain can get rid of it. Opponents of euthanasia tend to claim that pain can always be managed; proponents are equally adamant that the opposite is true. Despite great new advances to relieve pain and suffering, the actual delivery of that relief is, on the whole, sadly deficient. Doctors are often not well trained in pain control, and many of them tend to treat pain conservatively, both for fear of addicting their patients to analgesics and for fear that providing adequate pain relief may be seen as a form of euthanasia.

On the other hand, there is evidence that currently available measures are able to relieve the pain and suffering of almost every dying person. Adequate pain control is best provided when the patient is treated with an individualized care plan for pain and when an interdisciplinary palliative-care team (consisting of health care professionals and pastoral counselors) provides support. Although such care is increasingly being offered, especially in connection with the hospice movement, the need continues for improved training in pain management on the part of doctors and nurses.

Pain management and defusing the fear of pain and suffering are directly related to suicide and assisted suicide. As Kathleen Foley writes, "We frequently see patients referred to our Pain Clinic who have considered suicide as an option or who request physician-assisted suicide because of uncontrolled pain. We commonly see such ideation and requests dissolve with adequate control of pain and other symptoms, using combinations of pharmacologic, neurosurgical, anaesthetic, and psychological approaches" (as quoted in *Episcopal Diocese*, p. 52).

## Maintaining Dignity and Control

Besides fearing the pain and suffering that often accompany dying, most people feel an understandable apprehension about the loss of dignity and control that come with aging and with dying at any age. It is difficult to accept the loss of physical self-sufficiency and to accept with a measure of grace the indignities associated with the loss of bodily functions and mental faculties. A sense of helplessness and loss of self-esteem can severely aggravate a dying person's suffering, but the understanding and the loving support of a caring community can make a difference and provide much comfort for the dying person.

## Giving Life-Care Directives

Few of us want to look death in the face long enough to make decisions about it. But failure to do so usually means that health care professionals do whatever it takes to keep us alive—very possibly against our wishes and with little purpose. Therefore, we need to prepare clear instructions specifying the type of treatment we wish to receive when we are no longer capable of making such decisions. We need to engage our families in frank conversations about these things, and we need to provide them and potential caregivers with life-care directives, such as living wills and durable power of attorney for health care decisions. When we assume responsibility for these matters, we take the burden off our loved ones' shoulders—a burden that often leads to confusion, guilt, and conflict and that all too often can leave them in doubt about what to do.

Hospitals and nursing centers respect such instructions and often routinely ask for them. Many long-term care facilities—Christian institutions among them—stress the need, at the time of admission, for developing a care plan that includes these provisions. It is essential that these instructions are on file for retrieval when needed or are communicated to someone who is trustworthy and that these instructions are kept up to date. Up-to-date wills and clear instructions for funeral arrangements can further relieve the burden our death places on our families.

Who should decide which course of action should be followed? The person who is dying? A loved one? The medical staff? Or should this be a communal decision?

## Caring for the Caregivers

Providing care for a dying person is, for family members, a most exhausting task. The wife who lovingly attends her dying husband will eventually feel the strain. And children responsible for providing such care also find it hard to sustain long nights with little sleep. The family needs regular respite care, the care provided by a hospice agency or by trained nurse volunteers from within the church or community. But families who surround their loved ones in hospitals and nursing homes need respite too.

Many churches have instituted a parish-nurse program that matches the church's resources to various needs. Though smaller churches may not be able to achieve this level of coordination, some larger churches, especially those in urban centers, may well consider designating a trained person to coordinate such a ministry.

Respite care takes on many forms. It may take the form of child care, for example. Church members can offer meals, help with shopping, take over laundry, and do home cleaning chores. If a ramp is required, church members can be mobilized to build it. Deacons may sensitively offer to cover unexpected expenses. Someone might provide a recreational vehicle to allow the family to get away. The district elder walks along on this difficult journey by regularly stopping by to listen and to pray. Someone with links to these services may help connect children to grief-support groups such as Rainbows.

Our churches are filled with many gifted, caring members. They need only to be mobilized, their gifts coordinated. Sometimes the pastor may be the person to take the initiative. In many cases other believers will use this opportunity to share their gifts in this ministry.

## Supplying Hospice Care

Palliative care takes many forms. One of the more recent and most commendable is the hospice movement. This movement has precursors as far back in history as the Middle Ages, when pilgrims and crusaders found refuge in hospice shelters. Today the movement stands for a concept of care that helps people with dying—either at home or in a home-like setting away from home—in a way that ensures comfort, aggressively manages pain, and provides emotional and spiritual support. That support extends to the caregivers as well and, when needed, provides grief counseling following a loved one's death. Members of our churches would do well to acquaint themselves with the hospice ministries and to support them wholeheartedly.

## Developing the Educational Ministry of the Church

End-of-life issues provide their own teachable moments in the life of the church. The ministry of our members to families in crisis spurs us toward communal service and prayer. It can also prompt us to look into educational offerings that bring faith, health, and end-of-life issues together. These matters deserve to be lifted up in the preaching ministry of the church. They can also be emphasized in adult education programs.

Churches can access the local community for information and resources. Health care agencies will gladly provide the necessary resources.

## Suspending Judgment

We celebrate the lives of those who die at peace, especially when those who grieve the loss also experience acceptance and peace. Then we remember the life God gave and give thanks for the loved one who has died, for the grace of God in his or her life, and for our Christian hope.

But it is difficult to do that when people end their lives through choices that seem to us simply wrong or even tragic:

- when a friend stuns us with her suicide;

- when a Christian brother refuses to take nourishment and starves himself to death;

- when families choose to keep an aged parent on life support far longer than we would have done;

- when others shun life support and appear to hasten death.

End-of-life decisions are seldom as neat and tidy in practice as in theory. Some situations are difficult far beyond our comprehension. Some situations are so horrendous, so far beyond our comprehension that we need to suspend judgment. Especially then we need to point each other to God's grace.

Is "suspending judgment" the same thing as agreement? What's the difference?

## Point to Ponder

*From your own experience reflect on whether the concept of "Communities of Care" is a pie-in-the-sky concept. Give some concrete examples of why you believe you are or are not a part of such a community. How can you help to bring such a community into being or improve on it? Does that require individual action or a communal commitment? How will you proceed?*

# implications for public policy pertaining to the end of life

*How should government respond to end-of-life issues? In this section the report seeks to provide some answers based on Scripture. But the report's approach does not seem to dovetail with current trends. For example, the Netherlands became the first country in the world to enact legislation permitting assisted suicide. In November 2000, the Lower House of Parliament accepted a proposal that would permit physicians to play an active role in suicide when the following conditions are met:*

- *Independent commissions are to be formed consisting of a lawyer, a physician, and an ethicist whose approval must be sought before a doctor can proceed with euthanasia.*

- *The patient must have repeatedly and emphatically requested the attending physician's assistance in the euthanasia process.*

- *The patient must be incurably ill and suffer severe pain.*

- *The attending physician must consult another physician before he submits his/her request to the independent commission for approval.*

Do you think that by adopting this policy the Dutch government still adequately protects human life? Please explain.

*The proposal was accepted with a 104 to 40 vote majority. Among those opposing the proposal was the coalition of Protestant Christian and Roman Catholic members. The Upper House is expected to give its approval in the beginning of 2001. A recent survey in Belgium found that 81 percent of the population favors some form of assisted suicide.*

## Terminating Human Life Not an Option

As we said at the beginning of this report, we affirm our commitment to life as a gift of God. Life is a trust we are called to cherish and protect both in ourselves and in others. In the Latimer case that trust was broken when Tracy's father could no longer bear the burden of watching Tracy suffer. We acknowledge that sorrow, pain, indignity, or frustration may make life a heavy burden. But if we are true to our commitment, we must find ways of cherishing and protecting each person's life—even when that calls for a great deal of personal sacrifice, as in the case of Nigel Martin.

Responsible medical practice needs to be guided by a deep respect for the God-given value of human life. This value is not diminished by the physical or mental ravages of old age, disability, disease, accident, or deformity. We may not terminate life on the basis of any of these things, for doing so places us on the slippery slope of treating a life as a disposable commodity when its apparent usefulness is lost.

Our society must not accept assisted suicide or mercy killing as appropriate responses to the burden life may become. In keeping with this principle, we believe it is incumbent on the church to encourage government initiatives that protect the weak and vulnerable in society. This means that when private and community resources prove insufficient, as they so often do, government must provide adequate health care funding so that *all* persons can have full access to the necessary resources.

The role of the health care community is to help people overcome the distress of sickness, disability, and untimely death. But there comes a time at the close of every person's life when it is clear that even the most heroic medical efforts will no longer maintain life. In that dying stage the emphasis in medical care must be on securing the greatest possible level of comfort for the one who is dying rather than on seeking to extend that person's life as long as possible. Especially in this final phase of life, people are to be treated with the utmost respect. Respect for life at this stage does not mean that we deny patients further treatment nor that we leave them to suffer excruciating pain. Rather, it means that we, together with health care professionals, recognize and acknowledge the point at which our best efforts at providing care must shift from a curative emphasis to a palliative one.

## Legislation That Is Merciful and Just

Many of us have known people—perhaps in our own families—who suffered from a type of cancer that was accompanied by ferocious pain. We may have witnessed their extreme agony and may even have asked for or approved the administration of the level of morphine needed to control the unre-

It is estimated that there are between 10,000 and 25,000 adult patients in the United States who are in a persistent vegetative state. If Canada and the United States legalized assisted suicide, do you think that people would be more likely to accept ending the lives of such people because of the benefit of reduced health care costs?

lenting pain. And after that, we probably noticed that with the easing of the fiercest pain the patients' awareness of their surroundings receded until, finally, they slipped away into peaceful and painless death.

At such a time, who is to say with any degree of certainty that it was the increasing dosage of morphine that hastened or actually brought on the expected ultimate end? At a time like this, where the management of pain becomes the primary focus of care, the question hardly seems to matter.

But the question *does* matter, and it needs to be addressed.

We acknowledge that varying circumstances allow for a range of medical interventions that no one statute could possibly address. That is why the law must allow a measure of flexibility to accommodate some of the variables that may occur at the end of life. For example, no one would want to permit an accident victim with serious internal injuries simply to be taken off life support when death is not inevitable. In such a case every possible medical effort must be made to ensure survival and eventual recovery. But if a patient suffers from terminal cancer and is clearly in the dying stage, the situation is different. The physician must have the professional and legal freedom to treat the patient in a manner consistent with responsible medical practice.

When the moral and legal aspects of the matter become increasingly difficult, we need to draw on the expertise of the legal and medical professionals in our midst to guide us in our responses to these situations. The emphasis of care must be on providing the dying person with relief from unbearable pain. God's mercy is great enough to encompass this need, and God's people should be advocates of that mercy.

The Virginia-based National Hospice Organization runs some 1,800 hospice programs in the United States. Most of them are in or near large metropolitan areas. Placement is limited. Cost is between 20 to 40 percent below that of regular hospitals and is usually covered by Medicare and several private insurers. Hospice care focuses on pain control—preventing it, rather than relieving it on demand. Emotional and spiritual support is available to assist patients in coming to terms with terminal illness. The dying can count on the sympathetic hospice staff and volunteer visitors. Local Hospice units are often supported by churches whose representatives also may provide pastoral care where accepted. Limited counseling services are available for surviving relatives. Contact: The National Hospice Organization, 1901 North Fort Myer Dr., Suite 402, Arlington, VA 22209 or Southwest Christian Hospice, 7225 Lester Road, Union City, GA 30291.

In Canada the Canadian Palliative Care Association lists nearly six hundred hospice and palliative programs across the country. But the list includes regional health centers, long-term care institutions, and private nursing agencies that may or may not have palliative specialists. Canada has no nationally accepted standards of practice for hospice or palliative care. Unless they are affiliated with a hospital or accredited health center, community hospices are independent charitable corporations that run their own programs. For specific information, contact the Canadian Palliative Care Association, 131C - 43 Bruyere St., Ottawa, Ontario K1N 5C8; 613-241-3663; www.cpca.net.

How much flexibility should the law allow so that medical staff, loved ones, and dying persons themselves can make appropriate decisions?

49

New legislation may be needed to protect both doctors and patients in this final stage of life, for doctors may find themselves in conflict with the law when administering a treatment which, though aimed solely at relief of suffering and distress, may actually hasten the onset of death.

Elderly patients, on the other hand, must be assured that adequate controls are in place to guide and supervise the health care professionals who are giving treatment at this vulnerable stage of life. Presently there are many places in which there is neither adequate control within the health care system nor effective scrutiny from the medical community or the government. We fear that this deficiency could lead by default to medical practices that will fall outside of both legislation and the professional standards of medical ethics.

It was out of these concerns that in April 1995 the Committee for Contact with the Government (CCG) submitted its brief to Canada's Senate Special Committee on Euthanasia and Assisted Suicide. The brief specifically addressed the question "to what extent the process of dying may be shortened by medical treatment aimed at reducing suffering and ensuring a peaceful end."

Do good intentions matter? Does motive make a difference morally if the outcome is the same? For example, if our motive is to prevent pain but the treatment we provide shortens the patient's life, does it matter *what* we actually intended (only to subdue the pain or actually to hasten death)?

In its brief the CCG recommended legislative change that would permit medical intervention *only for the relief of pain and suffering* even if such treatment could shorten life when patients are clearly approaching the end of life. If such treatment would hasten death, the cause of death should be attributed to the originating disease and not to the treatment to relieve pain and suffering. The CCG further recommended legislation that would legally define and recognize a terminal phase of life that would be certified in consultations between the attending medical professionals and the patient or designated representatives.

In the United States, legal health care requirements vary from state to state. Therefore our committee would suggest that Christian Reformed congregations in the United States urge Christian health care and legal professionals, particularly those who are thoroughly familiar with their own states' health care systems, to prepare and submit similar recommendations that are appropriate to the jurisdictions within which the congregations are located.

Finally, the most vulnerable among us need protection from those who consider society's weakest members to be expendable. At a time when the skyrocketing cost of health care is straining financial resources to their very limits, it is particularly necessary to regulate medical practices to ensure that the lives of even the poorest and most marginalized among us are treated with the greatest compassion and the utmost respect.

## Point to Ponder

*Dr. Stanley Hauerwas, professor of theological ethics at the Divinity School of Duke University, Durham, North Carolina, states that modern medical science and technology is designed to safeguard and lengthen human life. That same medical know-how is administered to the elderly without much regard to whether its focus should be so much on lengthening life. He quotes a study that projects that by the year 2040 the elderly will constitute 21 percent of the general population—more if innovative medical technology continues to make strides. The elderly will consume at least 45 percent of all expenses for public health care. The total health expenses for the elderly are proportionately twice as high as for children. The irony is that by lengthening the human life span, chronic illnesses will increase, further reducing the quality of life.*

*When a normal life span has been lived out, Hauerwas concludes, medical sophistry should not be used to extend it. Hauerwas does not suggest how this might work in practice. The growing political power of senior citizens is also a factor. The problem is real: lengthening life span means more costly medical care. And that means less health funding for the young.*

*What do you think?*

# a call to action

*What follows are the actions that Synod 2000 of the Christian Reformed Church took in responding to this report and to its recommendations. Take some time to reflect on these as you think through the implications of what God calls us to do individually and communally to minister to a person whose life is rapidly drawing to an end and to his or her loved ones.*

**1. Synod receive[d] Sections 1-7 of the report from the Committee to Study Responsibility and Community at the End of Life as pastoral advice to the churches concerning care for the dying (with several amendments that have been incorporated in this version of the report).**

By adopting this as "pastoral advice," synod did not bind the churches to the content of this report but recommended it to them for their use. Did synod go far enough? Did it go too far?

**2. Synod urge[s] the churches to implement the following guidelines with regard to care for the dying:**

a. That with respect to empowering family members, churches

- encourage families to engage in frank discussions about the issues surrounding death and dying.
- encourage families to prepare advance directives regarding palliative care.
- encourage families, dying persons, and all caregivers to exercise their right and responsibility to be active members of the team for the care of the dying.

Are these five guidelines useful? Are they too narrow or too broad? Are they too weak or too tough? What's your opinion? *see 49, 50*

b. That with respect to their local community, churches

- identify and match community and congregational resources.
- form partnerships with community-care programs and agencies.
- encourage members to volunteer in local care programs, e.g., involve youth groups to assist seniors in the community.

c. That with respect to the health care community, churches

- encourage health care professionals to recognize that dying persons, their families, doctors, chaplains, pastors, and other caregivers constitute a team for care for the dying.
- encourage the medical community to give priority to effective pain management.
- encourage the medical community to develop and/or utilize an end-of-life care plan that goes beyond addressing the mere physical needs of the dying, e.g. hospice care.

d. That with respect to its members, churches

- preach and teach a biblical view of death as well as the gospel's hope of life after death.
- include in their ministry of prayer the dying, their families, and their caregivers.
- cherish and embrace in their church lives the disabled, the aged, the suffering, and those near the end of life.
- match gifts and needs in the congregation.
- encourage the recognition and development of caregiving skills.
- provide respite for caregivers.
- provide financial assistance where required.

e. That with respect to public policy, churches

- encourage the allocation of health care funding for adequate palliative services, home care, and medical support services for all people.
- encourage government initiatives that will allow medical treatment aimed at pain relief even if that treatment may unintentionally shorten life.
- encourage government initiatives that will promote life-affirming legislation and oppose legislation that endorses assisted suicide or mercy killing.

How do you think your church could address the government on these issues?

*3. Synod request[s] CRC Publications to publish educational materials on care for the dying, using the study report as amended and guidelines adopted above as appropriate.*

*Ground:* There is an urgent need for pastoral advice regarding communal care for the dying.

*4. Synod encourage[s] the churches to take note of and utilize the bioethics materials already marketed by CRC Publications and to make these materials available to their members as well as to health care professionals in their respective communities.*

## Point to Ponder
*Which of these guidelines should take priority in your church? How can your church begin to specifically implement those you choose? What will you do?*

For further study, contact Faith Alive Christian Resources (the education division of CRC Publications) at 1-800-333-8300 or e-mail us at sales@faithaliveresources.org for more educational materials on this topic.

# bibliography

The study committee appended this bibliography to its report. It suggests some excellent resources for further study.

Bouma, Hessel III, et al. *Christian Faith, Health, and Medical Practice*. Grand Rapids, MI: Eerdmans, 1989.

Byock, Ira. *Dying Well: Peace and Possibilities at the End of Life*. New York: Riverhead, 1997.

Clemons, James T. *What Does the Bible Say about Suicide?* Minneapolis: Fortress, 1990.

Cohen, Adam. "Showdown for Doctor Death." *Time*. 7 Dec. 1998: 26-27.

Committee for Contact with the Government, Christian Reformed Church in North America—Canadian Ministries Board. *Medical Decisions Pertaining to the End of Life: A Discussion Paper*; April 1995. (This paper was prepared for submission to the Canadian Senate Special Commission on Euthanasia and Assisted Suicide.)

Episcopal Diocese of Washington. Committee on Medical Ethics. *Assisted Suicide and Euthanasia: Christian Moral Perspectives*. Harrisburg, PA: Morehouse, 1997.

Eareckson Tada, Joni. *When Is It Right to Die? Suicide, Euthanasia, Suffering, Mercy*. Grand Rapids, MI: Zondervan, 1992.

Gentles, Ian, ed. *Euthanasia and Assisted Suicide, the Current Debate*. Toronto: Stoddard, 1995.

Gula, Richard M. *Euthanasia: Moral and Pastoral Perspectives*. Mahwah, NJ: Paulist, 1994.

Hamel, Ron, ed. *Choosing Death: Active Euthanasia, Religion, and Public Debate*. Philadelphia: Trinity, 1981.

Koop, C. Everett. *The Right to Live, the Right to Die*. Wheaton, IL: Tyndale, 1976.

May, William F. *Testing the Medical Covenant: Active Euthanasia and Health Care Reform*. Grand Rapids, MI: Eerdmans, 1996.

Morrow, Lance. "Time for the Ice Floe, Pop." *Time*. 7 Dec. 1998: 29.

Nuland, Sherwin B. *How We Die: Reflections on Life's Final Chapter*. New York: Knopf, 1994.

Vos, Mirth. *Letters to Myself on Dying*. Grand Rapids, MI: Baker and CRC Publications, 1999.

Wennberg, Robert N. *Terminal Choices: Euthanasia, Suicide, and the Right to Die*. Grand Rapids, MI: Eerdmans, 1989.